This Book
belongs to

....

....

....

WOMAN
A Unique Tribute

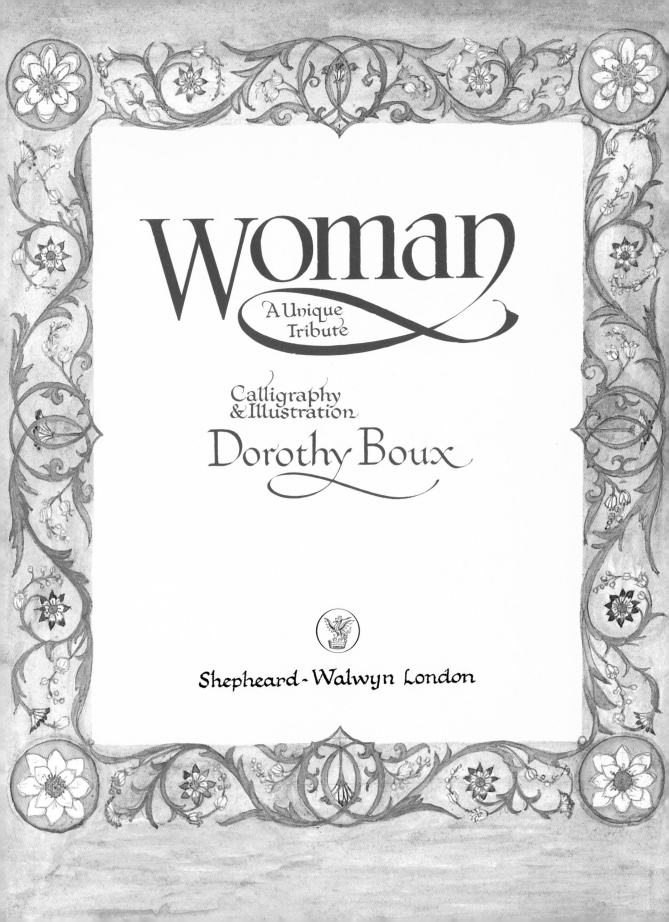

Woman

A Unique Tribute

Calligraphy
& Illustration
Dorothy Boux

Shepheard-Walwyn London

First published in 1999 by
Shepheard-Walwyn (Publishers) Ltd
26 Charing Cross Road (Suite 34)
London WC2H 0DH

ISBN 0 85683 183 2

Printed and bound in Singapore
by Craft Print Pte Ltd.

TABLE of CONTENTS

EVERYTHING IN CREATION STARTS FROM ONE,

and eventually returns to its source. Like the still point at the centre of the circle, it holds the myriad forms and sustains them. Fundamental to the established order, and one of the primary differentiations, the roles of masculine and feminine arise, carrying within them the power to generate, and to uphold and sustain each other.

It is said that the smallest unit of society is the family, and we have all at some time belonged to one. When the family works well happiness arises, when it is fragmented misery abounds. Central to the well-being of any family is a woman, whether she be mother, sister, wife or daughter. The woman is endowed by her very name and nature with the nurturing and supportive qualities out of which the very fabric of society is woven, and she can, if she remembers herself, play a large part in restoring and holding the balance.

Today, the need for such an effort on the part of woman is paramount. The innate strength which arises when the lady is in place can become available to all. Whether she finds herself running a home, teaching, or working in commerce; in fact whatever her function, she can make her inner resources available.

In exploring through these pages the true nature of woman, the experiences of her life, from youth and young love to maturity, and essentially in referring back to the bed-rock of the unity which lies at the root of creation, the lady may rediscover herself, her strength and her true purpose, and thus become of profound use to

EVERYONE

ŌM!

ADORATION TO THE DEITY!
UNDEFINABLE OMNIPOTENCY!
THE FOUNT OF UNIVERSAL ENERGY!
INFINITE INTELLIGENCE INCARNATE!

Lo! said the guru at whose feet I sat,
Thy essence is self-knowledge: Thou art That!
Seek for the key to thine own mystery
Within! Omniscience dwells in secrecy
In thine own heart. Without, what's that to thee?
Seek ye this 'I'. Drink at it's source, and then
Thou wilt eschew the ways of mortal men,
Who come and go in millions without ken,
Pursuing joys transitory and gross,
Discriminating not the gold from dross,
Each building in his ignorance his cross.
Let them their false gods serve, but learn thou this;
Self-knowledge only is eternal bliss.

BHARTRIHARI

'The purpose of any language is to tell the truth. The need of any listener is to be reminded of the truth within himself.'

IN THE BEGINNING... FROM the vibrant heart of the ONE, the bright dawn of light is manifested, the first movement of creation, which is itself an act of love. It carries on its wings of consciousness the essence of man; the begetter, the generator, the powerful, he who sets in motion. Enfolded within the man, close to his heart, like one half of a seed, is woman, the power which brings to birth, brings forth life, measures the universe.

Radiant with light, grounded in love, they sing a song of joy together, a song destined to sound in their hearts throughout all time.

CREATION

Sound of ether,

Touch of air,

Fire of form,

Flow of water,

Smell of earth.

So God created man in his own image, in the

ETERNAL WORD,
all wisdoms fruitful source,
Being without beginning, without end,
Light of all light, perfect in sympathy,
God worshipped in supreme divinity.
You, to make man in your own image, set
His mighty dwelling on the solid globe,
On this firm basis made his being move,
Created him with one almighty word.
You, to establish a thrice glorious throne,
Raised up the heavens about this humble earth,
And sowed their fields with everlasting fire.
Earth, the rough stage of human pride and greed;
Heaven, where your angels have no mortal need;
All is the fabric of
DIVINE DESIRE.
Jean Racine –

image of God created he him, male and female created he

them. And God blessed them, and God said unto them. Be fruit-

ful, and multiply, and replenish the earth, and subdue it.

3

IN THE BEGINNING THIS UNIVERSE WAS BUT THE SELF OF A HUMAN FORM. nothing else but He reflected, and found himself. He first uttered 'I AM HE'. Therefore he was called I. Hence, to this day, when a person is addressed, he first says 'It is I' and then says the other name that he may have...

HE WAS AFRAID. Therefore people still are afraid to be alone. He thought "If there is nothing else but me, what am I afraid of?" From that alone his fear was gone, for what was there to fear? It is from a second entity that fear comes.

HE WAS NOT AT ALL HAPPY

4

Therefore people still are not happy
when alone. He desired a mate...
Brihad Upanishad

AND THE LORD GOD SAID,

It is not good that man should be alone;
I will make him an help meet for him...

AND the Lord God caused a deep sleep to fall
upon Adam, and he slept; and he took one
of his ribs, and closed up the flesh thereof;

AND the rib which the Lord God had taken
from man, made he a woman, and brought
her unto the man.

AND Adam said, This is now bone of my
bones, and flesh of my flesh: she shall be called
Woman, because she was taken out of Man.
Genesis

Therefore...this body is one half of oneself
LIKE ONE OF THE TWO HALVES
OF A SPLIT PEA *Brihad-Upanishad*

THE DAYLIGHT ✳ ✳lingered past its time
In rose-leaf radiance   on the watching peaks,
So that it seemed   Night listened in the glens
And noon upon   ✳the mountains; Yea, they write,
The Evening   ✳stood between them like some
Celestial,   love~struck, rapt;   maid
   ✳   the smooth-rolled clouds
Her braided hair, the studded stars the pearls
   And diamonds of her coronal; the moon
Her forehead jewel, and the deepening dark
   S✳   her woven garments...
                              Light of Asia
   SHE✳ was a Phantom of delight
When first she gleam'd upon my sight
   A lovely Apparition, sent
   To be a moment's ornament;
Her eyes as stars of ✳twilight fair;
Like Twilight's too, her dusky hair;
But all things else about her drawn
From May-time and the cheerful dawn;
   A dancing shape, and image gay,
   To haunt, to startle, and waylay.

I saw her upon nearer view,
A Spirit, yet a Woman too!
Her household motions light and free,
And steps of virgin-liberty;
A countenance in which did meet
Sweet records, promises as sweet;
A creature not too bright or good
For human nature's daily food,
For transient sorrows, simple wiles,
Praise, blame, love, kisses, tears, and smiles.

And now I see with eye serene
The very pulse of the machine;
A being breathing thoughtful breath,
A traveller between life and death:
The reason firm, the temperate will,
Endurance, foresight, strength, and skill;
A perfect Woman, nobly plann'd
To warn, to comfort, and command;
And yet a Spirit still, and bright
With something of an angel-light.

William Wordsworth

WOMAN

~was created from the rib of man,

Not from his head to top him,

Neither from his feet to be walked upon,

She was made from his side to be at
ONE with him,

From near his heart to be loved by him.

After St Thomas Aquinas ~

8

LIGHT

my light, the world-filling light, the eye-kissing
light, heart-sweetening light! Ah, the light dances,
my darling, at the centre of my life; the light strikes,
my darling, the chords of my love; the sky opens,
the wind runs wild, laughter passes over the earth.
The butterflies spread their sails on the sea of light
Lilies and jasmines surge up on the crest of the
waves of light. The light is shattered into gold on
every cloud, my darling, and it scatters gems in
profusion. Mirth spreads from leaf to leaf, my
darling, and gladness without measure. The heaven's
river has drowned its banks and the flood of joy
is abroad.

Rabindranath Tagore

9

INSIGHT VAST

Ranging beyond this sphere to spheres unnamed,
 System on system, countless worlds and suns
Moving in splendid measures, band by band
Linked in division, ONE, yet separate,
The silver islands of a sapphire sea
Shoreless, unfathomed, undiminished, stirred
With waves which roll in restless tides of change.

He saw those LORDS OF LIGHT who hold their worlds
By bonds invisible, how they themselves
 Circle obedient round mightier orbs
Which serve profounder splendours, star to star
Flashing the ceaseless radiance of life
 From centres ever shifting unto cirques
 Knowing no uttermost.
        Light of Asia

Yea, the first Morning of Creation wrote
What the Last Dawn of Reckoning shall read...
            Rubaiyat - Omar Khayam

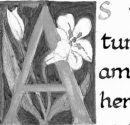S the wheels of lives begin to turn, the lady asks herself 'Who am I?' and from the depths of her own being, comprehends the meaning of her name.

'She who has true knowledge, who measures the universe; power, ability, and serenity; the stream of life, nourisher and sustainer; beauty, grace and goodness; the bearer of children'.

Even as she gazes in wonder at her own true nature, the clouds gather about her, and with the passage of time they begin to cover her true light. But the man remembers and shelters the flame with his presence, calling upon his mate to strengthen and support him on the path of life.

MY NATURE IS KNOWLEDGE

WOMAN KNOW THYSELF.

AND NOTHING OTHER THAN KNOWLEDGE ✳ VERILY THE UNIVERSE IS REVEALED UNDER THE LIGHT OF MYSELF ✳

I AM she that is the natural mother of all things, mistress and governess of all the elements, the initial progeny of worlds, chief of the powers divine, queen of all that are in hell, the principal of them that dwell in heaven, manifested alone and under one form of all the gods and goddesses. At my will the planets of the sky, the wholesome winds of the seas, and the lamentable silences of hell are disposed; my name, my divinity is adored throughout the world, in divers manners, in variable customs, and by many names.

For the Phrygians that are the first of all men call me the Mother of the gods of Pessinus; the Athenians, which are sprung from their own soil, Cecropian Minerva; the Cyprians, which are girt about by the sea, Paphian Venus; the Cretans, which bear arrows, Dictynian Diana; the Sicilians, which speak three tongues, infernal Proserpine; the Eleusians their ancient goddess Ceres; some Juno, others Bellona, others Hecate, others Ramnusie, and principally both sort of the Ethiopians, which dwell in the Orient and are enlightened by the morning rays of the sun; and the Egyptians, which are excellent in all kind of ancient doctrine, and by their proper ceremonies accostomed to worship me, do call me by my true name, Queen Isis.

BEHOLD I AM COME TO TAKE PITY OF THY FORTUNE AND TRIBULATION; BEHOLD I AM PRESENT TO FAVOUR AND AID THEE; LEAVE OFF THY WEEPING AND LAMENTATION, PUT AWAY ALL THY SORROW, FOR BEHOLD THE HEALTHFUL DAY WHICH IS ORDAINED BY MY PROVIDENCE.

Lucius Apuleius

13

14

In Sanskrit, the root language of all languages, woman, the embodiment of the feminine principle in Creation, is defined thus: divine Mother, tranquility, peace, constancy, contentment, one who measures and supports, knower of true knowledge, ability, strength, beauty, splendour, honour and glory.

AND without partiality, a woman of sense and manners is the finest and most delicate part of God's creation, the glory of her Maker, and the great instance of his singular regard to man, his darling creature, to whom he gave the best gift, either that God could bestow or man receive.

A woman well-bred and well-taught, furnished with the additional accomplishments of knowledge and behaviour, is a creature without comparison.

Daniel Defoe

15

I
SAW
ETERNITY
LIKE A GREAT RING OF PURE
AND ENDLESS LIGHT,
THE OTHER NIGHT,

And God said
eat of the
tree which is
of the
So when the
that the tree
for food ...she
fruit and ate,
gave some to her
ate. Then the eyes of

'You shall not
fruit of the
in the midst
garden...
woman saw
was good
took of its
and she also
husband, and he
both were opened...
Genesis

ALL CALM, AS   IT WAS BRIGHT;
And round beneath it, TIME, in hours, days, years,
Driven by the spheres, Like a vast shadow moved;
in which the world, and all her train were hurl'd.
Henry Vaughan

I took one draught of life
I'll tell you what I paid
Precisely an existence
The market price, they said.
Emily Dickinson

For in and out, above, about, below, 'Tis nothing but a
Magic Shadow~show, Played in a box whose Candle
is the Sun, Round which we Phantom Figures come and go.
Omar Khayam

16

She is
older than the rocks a-
mong which she sits; like the
vampire, she has been dead many times,
and learned the secrets of the grave; and
has been a diver in deep seas, and keeps
their fallen day about her; and trafficked for
strange webs with eastern merchants, and as
Leda, was the mother of Helen of Troy, and as
St. Anne, the mother of Mary; and all this has
been to her but as the sound of lyres and
flutes, and lives only in the delicacy with
which it has moulded the changing
lineaments and tinged the eyelids
and the hands.

Walter Pater ~

17

BE not ashamed, woman - your privilege
encloses the rest,
And is the exit of the rest,
You are the gates of the body, and you are
the gates of the soul. *Walt Whitman*

I AM that which began;
Out of me the years roll;
I am equal and whole;
God changes, and man, and the form of them bodily;
I am the soul. *Algernon C. Swinburne*

Ah, love, let us be true
To one another! for the world, which seems
To be be before us like a land of dreams,
So various, so beautiful, so new,
Hath really neither joy, nor love, nor light,
Nor certitude, nor peace, nor help for pain,
And we are here as on a darkling plain
Swept by confused alarms of struggle and flight,
WHERE IGNORANT ARMIES
CLASH BY NIGHT.
Matthew Arnold

TODAY

CHANGE arises out of the dissolution of the old form in order to allow the growth of the new. At such times the lady particularly needs to make her sustaining and regulating qualities available for the measuring of change and to maintain the balance. Only a full and generous giving can heal the wounds society inflicts upon itself. Open the newspapers on any day and read about the damaged lives, broken families, and human suffering that have become our daily bread. In order to effectively counteract this downward spiral, the lady must first find the true balance within herself, the fine point of the fulcrum that equalises both sides. Meditation, attention and devotion will lead her to her own inner stillness.

We no longer believe in an objective moral order. Instead we think of the good as something to be pursued individually rather than sought collectively.

DEAL AT KNIFEPOINT

THE ⚜ TIMES

the sake of the children conceals adult selfishness. It would be to reverse the reforms of the 1960s, which made divorce ut it is reasonable, knowing what we now do about the effects, to reconsider the whole question.

When one in four children is born outside marriage, when one child in three grows up without a father, when four marriages in ten end in divorce, when the very concept of parental responsibility is seen as an affront to women's right to pursue careers and men's right to pursue their inclinations, when the responsibility for socialising and controlling children has been abdicated in favour of the state in the form of schools, councils and the police, what shall some children do not to turn to crime ?

drugs

Above all, we are in danger of witnessing the end of the family as a stable and persisting unit through which future generations are nurtured and internalise the rules we have so painfully arrived at on our collective journey through history.

The very large increase in the rate of divorce is also a clear threat to the family.

In a d... consequences of this programme.

one of the consequences has been a rise in crime among the young, *how could it be otherwise,*

Quite apart from the deprivations of children growing up with only one parent, she considers the more immediate effect on their dispossessed biological fathers. What we are producing, she suggests, are the conditions for creating a new " warrior class " of men cut off from the socialising influence of family and domestic responsi... "large numbers of unattaches males for whom ... predatory sexual behaviour and ... property ". The decline of heav... working-class men unemployabl... social reformers to put them beyo... Detached from any sense of conti... these rogue males are becoming o... community. I go further than Patri... doom : it is probably only a matter ... demagogue sets out to organise this ...quency. In their alienation and unchecked aggressiveness, these displaced men are ideal fodder for fascist recruitment.

A society in which the whole burden of law and order is placed on the police, the law courts and parliament is unsustainable. It cannot be done, nor should we wish it to be done.

war

We are now approaching an era when the need to awaken and transform our consciousness is being felt all over the world. At no time has a re-emergence of the feminine been so urgently needed in order to create balance, harmony and peace on earth, in accord with the creative energies of nature.   Marija Gimbutas

Commandments are out of fashion in the permissive world society of today. That is because absolutes are out of fashion. There is generally no belief in absolute truth or absolute untruth; absolute right or absolute wrong; absolute beauty, absolute justice, absolute mercy or absolute standards in anything.

Instead, everything is relative: and related, usually, to what the individual likes or dislikes, wants or does not want...

As a result, what used to be the first lesson for the children of a western community - the Ten Commandments ~ has disappeared from the curriculum. A mixture of Marxist philosophy and Freudian psychology has persuaded the mind of the west that human beings are not responsible for their own actions and should not be expected to exercise restraint. They should neither restrain their own desires, nor those of their children. To prove the efficacy of this thinking, there is, of course, a mounting crime wave all through Europe and movements to establish the rights of children over their parents. Sheila Rosenberg

The lady determines both the measures in the community in which she lives and also the subtle substance or atmosphere within which they have their existence. When she is measured and her substance is unadulterated she is rightly reverenced and treated like a goddess. When she is unmeasured, she is reduced in the eyes of the community until she is little more than an object of desire.

Sheila Rosenberg

The contemporary womans liberation drive towards a decrease in sexual differentiation, to the extent that it is leading toward androgyny and unisexual values implies a social and cultural death-wish and the end of the civilisation that endorses it. The scientific and historical records show that all the way from unicellular organisms to human beings, progress in evolution has been stimulated by an increase in sexual differentiation.

Amaury de Reincourt

The ultimate unit for economic considerations is the family, which accounts for all individuals, bound together with love, affection and sacrifice. Happiness of a family depends upon the cultural, religious and philosophical traditions of the society. When cultural, religious and philosophical traditions become weak, the disintegration of the family begins. Individuals become greedy for security. Once general greed takes over, the economic structure begins to crack.

Shantand Saraswati

LET US LOOK AT THE EARTH AROUND US.

What is happening under our eyes within the mass of peoples? What is the cause of this disorder in society, this uneasy agitation, these swelling waves, these whirling and mingling currents and these turbulent and formidable new impulses? Mankind is visibly passing through a crisis of growth. Mankind is becoming dimly aware of its shortcomings and its capacities. And it sees the universe growing luminous like the horizon just before sunrise. It has a sense of premonition and of expectation.

Pierre Teilhard de Chardin

Whenever there is a withering of the law and an uprising of lawlessness on all sides, then I manifest Myself.
For the salvation of the righteous and the destruction of such as do evil, for the firm establishing of the Law, I come to birth age after age.

Bhagavad Gita

he women-folk, as they are empowered by their nature, respond much to the heart and the emotional aspect of their being is charged with much more energy compared to men, and they will keep on working only through that aspect in their life. Since the energy is there and the desire to be active in work related to that emotional aspect of their life is also there, the work may turn in any direction. It would be necessary to bring them to a point of stillness and steadiness in their being. If the steadiness is not materialised, if the inner realm of being is not referred to, then their energies could easily be dissipated in works that are not necessarily useful and they will lose everything, whatever they have, and this will lead to spiritual degradation.

Shantanand Saraswati

nce an old woman came to Buddha and asked him how to meditate. He told her to remain aware of every movement of hands as she drew the water from the well, knowing that if she did, she would soon find herself in that state of alert and spacious calm that is meditation. The practice of mindfulness, of bringing the scattered mind home, and so of bringing the different aspects of our being into focus, is called "Peacefully Remaining" or "Calmly Abiding". "Peacefully Remaining" accomplishes three things. First, all the fragmented aspects of ourselves, which have been at war, settle and dissolve and become friends. In

24

that settling we begin to understand ourselves more, and sometimes even have glimpses of the radiance of our fundamental nature.

Second, the practice of mindfulness defuses our negativity, aggression, and turbulent emotions, which may have been gathering power over many lifetimes. Rather than suppressing emotions or indulging in them, here it is important to view them, and your thoughts, and whatever arises with an acceptance and generosity that has the flavour of boundless space...

Third, this practice unveils and reveals your essential good Heart, because it dissolves and removes the unkindness or the harm in you. Only when we have removed the harm in ourselves do we become truly useful to others. Through the practice, then, by slowly removing the unkindness and harm from ourselves, we allow our true Good Heart, the fundamental goodness and kindness that are our real nature, to shine out and become the warm climate in which our true being flowers.   Sogyal Rinpoche

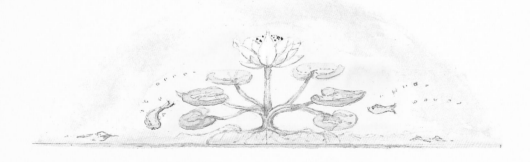

25

NOT I, NOT I, BUT THE WIND
THAT BLOWS THROUGH ME!
A fine wind is blowing the new
                    direction of Time.
If only I let it bear me, carry me,
                    if only it carry me,
If only I am sensitive, subtle, oh, delicate, a winged gift!
If only most lovely of all, I yield myself and am
                    borrowed
By the fine, fine wind that takes its course through
          the chaos of the world
Like a fine, an exquisite chisel, a wedge-blade inserted;
If only I am keen and hard like the sheer tip
                    of a wedge
          Driven by invisible blows,
The rock will split, we shall come at the wonder,
          we shall find the Hesperides.
Oh, for the wonder that bubbles into my soul;
I would be a good fountain, a good well-head,
    Would blur no whisper, spoil no expression.
          What is the knocking?
What is the knocking at the door in the night?
          It is somebody wants to do us harm.

NO, NO, IT IS THE THREE STRANGE ANGELS.
ADMIT THEM. ADMIT THEM.

D. H. Lawrence

26

AWAKE, AWAKE,

the world is young
_For all its weary years of thought.
The starkest fights must still be fought,
The most surprising songs be sung.

James Elroy Flecker

There are nine requisites for contented living.
Health enough to make work a pleasure; wealth
enough to support your needs; strength enough
to battle with difficulties and forsake them;
grace enough to confess your sins and over-
come them; patience enough to toil until some
good is accomplished; charity enough to see some
good in your neighbours; love enough to make
you useful and helpful to others; faith enough
to make real the things of God; hope enough
to remove all anxious fears concerning the future.

Johann Wolfgang von Goethe

It is only through that still point that the
effectiveness of women is possible. They
will become serious, loving and effect-
ive in their action due to the stillness
within and be of profound use to everyone.

Shantanand Saraswati

27

OUR DEEPEST FEAR IS NOT THAT WE ARE INADEQUATE.

OUR DEEPEST FEAR IS THAT WE ARE POWERFUL BEYOND MEASURE.

IT IS OUR LIGHT, NOT OUR DARKNESS, THAT MOST FRIGHTENS US.

We ask ourselves, "Who am I to be brilliant, gorgeous, talented, fabulous?"

Actually, who are you not to be? You are a child of God—.

Your playing small doesn't serve the world. There's nothing enlightened about shrinking so that other people won't feel insecure around you.

We are all meant to shine as children do. We are born to manifest the glory of God that is within us.

It's not just in some of us; it's in everyone.

And as we let our own light shine, we unconsciously give other people permission to do the same. As we're liberated from our own fear, our presence— automatically liberates others.

Nelson Mandela

28

LOVE

 **The** lady's innate knowledge of her own true nature and function needs to be acknowledged at an early stage, in order to allow a sound basis for the education and upbringing of daughters. Linked to a spiritual awareness of the foundation of all life, it will create a mainspring of strength from which the young lady can sustain a balanced course through the turbulent waters of adolescence and young love, in which she plays a major part.

Training and disciplining girls would be the most fruitful. If one took care of the girls, the boys would behave themselves. So establishing a good appreciation of measure related to every walk of life in the minds of girls is most necessary. India, since ancient times, has held women in great respect. First of all the concept of goddesses like Shakti, Lakshmi, etc. are associated with women...
It seems that if a reverence and honour for the womanhood is created in the minds of people, their attitude would change.   Shantanand Saraswati

Liberation movements, so-called, arise when women lose confidence in the significance of their function. It is no help to them, at such periods, to pretend that their function is other than it is. The ancient symbol of that function is woman seated in the lap of the Absolute, at the heart of the creation, looking out upon it, with the gaze of one who cares: in order to discern and meet the needs of the creation in all three worlds. What more could any woman want than that?
Within that function, which demands an intelligent mind, wakeful awareness, penetration, accomplishments, efficiency, service and perseverance, all conversation

about a girl's education and development should take
place. The measure of what one may tell a daughter lies,
not in parental awareness of their own shortcomings, but
IN TRUTH ITSELF. ~
Sheila Rosenberg   ~

SPRING WATER is most
healing and most inspiring,
because it comes from above
and runs downhill. That is
the character of the inspired
mind. The heart that like
a spring pours out water
in the form of inspiration,
in poetry or music or some
other form; has beauty,
has a healing quality.
It does take away all
the worries and anxieties
and difficulties and troubles
of those who come to it,
like the water of the
spring; it not only
inspires but it heals.

AGAIN,
  there is the water of a large pool,
    where water-lilies grow, where fish
      swim, where the sun is reflected
        and where moonlight produces a
      beautiful vision, where one would
  like to sit and look at it; because
it expresses to everyone that
can see it the liquid nature
  of the heart, the heart that
    is not frozen, the heart that
      is like water. It is still, it is
        calm. Sitting by its side can
        make one's heart
      tranquil and because
of its stillness one can
see one's reflection in it.
              Inayat Khan

Above all, hands are for prayer...

GOD SPEAKS

My child, it is not necessary to know much to please me; it is sufficient to love much. Speak to me as thou wouldst to a father if he drew near.

Are there any for whom thou wouldst pray to me? Repeat to me the names of thy relations, thy friends; after each name add what thou wouldst have me do for them. Ask much, ask much; I love generous souls who forget themselves for others.

Tell me of the poor thou wouldst relieve, the sick whom thou hast seen suffer, the sinners thou wouldst have converted, those who are alienated from thee, whose affection thou wouldst regain.

Are there graces thou wouldst ask for thyself? Write, if thou wilt, a long list of what thou desirest, of all the needs of thy soul, and come and read it to me.

Tell me simply how proud thou art, how sensitive, egotistical, mean and indolent. Poor child, do not blush; there are in heaven many saints who had their faults; they prayed to me, and little by little their faults were corrected.

Do not hesitate to ask me for blessings for the body and mind; for health, memory, and success. I can give you all things, and I always give, when my blessings are needed to render souls more holy.

Today what wilt thou have, my child? If thou knowest how I long to do thee good! Hast thou plans that occupy thee? Lay them all before me. Dost thou wish to give pleasure to thy mother, to thy family, to those on whom thou dost depend? What wouldst thou do for them?

And for me? Hast thou no zealous thought for me? Dost thou not wish to do a little good to the souls of thy friends who have perhaps forgotten me?

34

Bring me all thy failures, and I will show thee the cause of
them. Hast thou not troubles? Who has caused thee pain? Tell
me all. And wilt thou not end by adding that thou wilt pardon
and forget? ~ and I will bless thee...   Mediaeval

I thank Thee,
Heavenly Father,
because Thou hast put me
at a source of running streams,
at a living spring in a land of drought,
Watering an eternal garden of wonders,
the Tree of Life, mystery of mysteries,
growing everlasting branches for eternal planting
to send their roots into the stream of life
From an eternal source.
And Thou, Heavenly Father
protect their fruits
with the angels of the day
and of the night
and with flames of eternal Light
burning every way.

DEAD
SEA SCROLLS

Most girls start dreaming about marriage and the dream-figure they would like to marry at twelve or thirteen or fourteen...

THE ANCIENT INDIAN tradition places woman on three levels according to their age. From birth to the age of sixteen, a girl is addressed as daugter, from sixteen to thirty or thirty-two, she is addressed as sister, and from thirty-two on, she is addressed as mother. Most of the reasonable men still practice this. Once you bind yourself to these relationships, there arises a natural restraint.

Shantanand Saraswati

NATURE HAS GIVEN hearts to bulls, hoofs to horses, swiftness to hares, the power of swimming to fishes, of flying to birds, understanding to men. She had nothing more for woman save beauty. Beauty is proof against spears and shields. She who is beautiful is more formidable than fire or iron.

ANACREON

SHE BEGAN TO SING

Happy in beauty, life, and love and everything,
A song of love, too sweet for earthly lyres,
While, like held breath, the stars drew in their
panting fires.

John Keats

Had I the heaven's embroidered cloths,
Enwrought with golden and silver light;
The blue, the dim and the dark cloths—
I would spread these cloths under your feet;
But I being poor have only my dreams;
I have spread my dreams under your feet,
Tread softly, you tread on my dreams.

W. B. Yeats

AND HE REPLIED....

37

There be none of Beauty's daughters
    With a magic like Thee;
And like music on the waters
    Is thy sweet voice to me:
When, as if its sound were causing
    The charmed ocean's pausing,
The waves lie still and gleaming,
And the lull'd winds seem dreaming:

And the midnight moon is weaving
    Her bright chain o'er the deep,
Whose breast is gently heaving
    As an infant's asleep:
So the spirit bows before thee
    To listen and adore thee;
With a full but soft emotion,
Like the swell of Summer's ocean.

Lord Byron

38

Of all the girls that are so smart
There's none like pretty Sally;
She is the darling of my heart
And she lives in our alley.
There is no lady in the land
Is half so sweet as Sally;
She is the darling of my heart,
And she lives in our alley.

Her father he makes cabbage-nets
And through the streets does cry 'em;
Her mother she sells laces long
To such as please to buy 'em:
But sure such folks could ne'er beget
So sweet a girl as Sally!
She is the darling of my heart,
And she lives in our alley.

When she is by, I leave my work,
I love her so sincerely;
My master comes like any Turk,
And bangs me most severely ~
But let him bang his bellyful,
I'll bear it all for Sally;
She is the darling of my heart
And she lives in our alley.

Of all the days that's in the week
I dearly love but one day ~
And that's the day that comes betwixt
A Saturday and a Monday;
For then I'm drest all in my best
To walk abroad with Sally
She is the darling of my heart,
And she lives in our alley.

H. Carey

Tell me where is Fancy bred,
Or in the heart, or in the head?
How begot, how nourishéd?
Reply, reply.

It is engender'd in the eyes;
With gazing fed; and Fancy dies
In the cradle where it lies;
Let us all ring Fancy's knell;
I'll begin it, – Ding, dong, bell,
~ Ding, dong, bell.

William Shakespeare

The sea hath many thousand sands,
The sun has motes as many;
The sky is full of stars, and Love
As full of woes as any:
Believe me, that do know the elf,
And make no trial by thyself!

It is in truth a pretty toy
For babes to play withal : ~
But O! the honeys of our youth
Are oft our age's gall!
Self-proof in time will make thee know
He was a prophet told thee so;

A prophet that, Cassandra-like,
Tells truth without belief;
For headstrong Youth will run his race
Although his goal be grief: ~
Love's martyr, when his heat is past,
Proves Care's Confessor at the last.

                              Anon

THE TEMPLE BELLS ARE RINGING,
The young green corn is springing,
And the marriage month is drawing very near.
I lie hidden in the grass,
And I count the moments pass,
For the month of marriages is drawing near.

Soon, ah, soon, the women spread
The appointed bridal bed
With hibiscus buds and crimson marriage flowers,
Where, when all the songs are done,
And the dear dark night begun,
I shall hold her in my happy arms for hours.

She is young and very sweet,
From the silver on her feet
To the silver and the flowers in her hair,
And her beauty makes me swoon,
As the Moghra trees at noon
Intoxicate the hot and quivering air.

The Moghra flowers, the Moghra flowers,
So dear to Youth at play;
The small and subtle Moghra flowers
That only last a day."

Valgowind

The fields are full of Poppies, and the skies are very blue,
By the Temple in the coppice, I wait, Beloved, for you.
The level land is sunny, and the errant air is gay,
With scent of rose and honey, will you come to me today?

From carven walls above me, smile lovers; many a pair.
"Oh, take this rose and love me!" she has twined it in her hair.
He advances, she retreating, pursues and holds her fast,
The sculptor left them meeting, in a close embrace at last.

Through centuries together, in the carven stone they lie,
In the glow of golden weather, and endless azure sky.
Oh, that we, who have for pleasure so short and scant a stay,
Should waste our summer leisure; will you come to me today?

The Temple bells are ringing, for the marriage month
                                    has come,
I hear the women singing, and the throbbing of the drum.
And when the song is failing, or the drums a moment
                                    mute,
The wierdly wistful wailing of the melancholy flute.

Valgowind

This temple was older than its gods.
They remained, prisoners in the
temple, but the temple was far more
ancient. It had thick walls and
pillars in the corridors, carved with
horses, gods and angels. They had a
certain quality of beauty, and as you
passed them you wondered what
would happen if they all came alive,
including the innermost god.
They said that this temple, especially
the innermost sanctuary, went back
far beyond the imagination of time.
As you wandered through the
various corridors, lit by the morning sun and with sharp, clear shadows,
you wondered what it was all about.
Krishnamurti

44

SO OFTEN WE WANT HAPPINESS, but the very way we pursue it is so clumsy and unskilled that it only brings more sorrow. Usually we assume we must grasp in order to have that something that will ensure our happiness. We ask ourselves: How can we possibly enjoy anything if we cannot own it? How often attachment is mistaken for love! Even when the relationship is a good one, love is spoiled by attachment, with its insecurity, possessiveness and pride; and then when love is gone, all you are left to show for it are the "souvenirs" of love, the scars of attachment.

Sogyal Rinpoche

People of Orphalese, of what can I speak save of that which is even now moving within your souls?
Then said Almitra, Speak to us of Love.
And he raised his head and looked upon the people, and there fell a stillness upon them. And with a great voice he said:

WHEN love beckons to you, follow him,
Though his ways are hard and steep.
And when his wings enfold you
yield to him,
Though the sword hidden among his pinions may wound you.
And when he speaks to you believe in him,
Though his voice may shatter your dreams as the north wind lays waste the garden.
For even as love crowns you so shall he crucify you. Even as he is for your growth so is he for your pruning.
Even as he ascends to your height and caresses your tenderest branches that quiver in the sun,
So shall he descend to your roots and shake them in their clinging to the earth.

46

Like sheaves of corn he gathers you unto himself.
He threshes you to make you naked.
He sifts you to free you from your husks.
He grinds you to whiteness.
He kneads you until you are pliant;
And then he assigns you to his sacred fire, that
you may become sacred bread for God's sacred feast.

All these things shall love do unto you that you
may know the secrets of your heart, and in that
knowledge become a fragment of Life's heart.

Khalil Gibran

ONE has to discover the source which
is love and all the relationships by
which all things have their being.
Mother, father, sister, brother, colleague
and all relationships have some aspect
of love. One needs only to learn and respond
naturally to these relationships in their proper
sense. Simple and truthful relation is all we
need to maintain.

Shantanand Saraswati

And seeing in the water a shape, a shape like
unto himself, in himself he loved it, and would
cohabit with it...Nature presently laying hold
of what it so much loved, did wholly wrap herself about it, and they were mingled, for they
loved one another.
Hermes Trismegistus

When two people are at one in their
          inmost hearts,
They shatter even the strength of iron or bronze.
And when two people understand each other
          in their inmost hearts,
Their words are sweet and strong, like the
          fragrance of orchids.
          Chinese Tradition

For woman is increasingly aware that love
alone can give her full stature, just as the man
begins to discern that spirit alone can endow
his life with its highest meaning. Fundamentally,
therefore, both seek a psychic relation one to
the other, because love needs the spirit, and
the spirit love, for their fulfillment.
          Carl Gustav Jung

Love is all-pervading. It penetrates every-
where and it is unitary. It is one. Love is felt
between two or more and that is what brings
them together, and yet it is felt as unifying.
It removes the difference. The love between the
so-called two is one.
          Shantanand Saraswati

49

Then Almitra spoke again and said, And what of Marriage, master?
And he answered saying:
  You were born together, and together you shall be for evermore.
  You shall be together when the white wings of death
  scatter your days.
  Aye, you shall be together even in the silent memory
  of God.
  But let there be spaces in your togetherness.
And let the winds of the heavens dance between you.

  Love one another, but make not a bond of love:
  Let it rather be a moving sea between the shores of
  your souls.
  Fill each other's cup but drink not from one cup.
Give one another of your bread but eat not from the same
loaf.
  Sing and dance together and be joyous, but let each one of
you be alone,
Even as the strings of a lute are alone though they quiver with
the same music.

  Give your hearts, but not into each other's keeping.
  For only the hand of Life can contain your hearts
  And stand together yet not too near together:
  For the pillars of the temple stand apart,
  And the oak tree and the cypress grow not in each
  other's shadow.

                    Khalil Gibran

Come, my friend, to greet the bride,
to welcome in the Sabbath eve.

'Observe!', 'Remember!' ~ one command,
God made us hear a single phrase.
For He is one, His name is one,
in fame, in glory and in praise.
Come, my friend, to greet the bride,
to welcome in the Sabbath eve.

To greet the Sabbath let us join
for from her endless blessings pour;
First of all creation willed,
the final act, thought long before.
Come, my friend, to greet the bride,
to welcome in the Sabbath eve.

Arouse yourself, arouse yourself,
your light is come, arise and shine!
Awake, awake and pour out song,
God's glory greets us at this time
Come, my friend, to greet the bride,
to welcome in the Sabbath eve.

Come in peace and come in joy,
God, your husband; you, His pride;
among the faithful chosen people,
come my bride, come my bride!
Come, my friend, to greet the bride,
to welcome in the Sabbath eve.
Alkabetz

MARRIAGE THOUGHTS

Bridegroom:

I give you my house and my lands, all golden with harvest,
My sword, my shield and my jewels, the spoils of my strife,
My strength and my dreams, and ought I have gathered
of glory,
And to-night ~ to-night, I shall give you my very life.

Bride:

I may not raise my eyes, oh my Lord, towards you,
And I may not speak: what matter? my voice would fail,
But through my downcast lashes, feeling your beauty,
I shiver and burn with pleasure beneath my veil.

Younger Sisters:

We throw sweet perfumes upon her head,
And delicate flowers round her bed.
Ah, would that it were our turn to wed!

Mother:

I see my daughter, vaguely, through my tears,
(Ah, lost caresses of my early years!)
I see the bridegroom, King of men in truth!
(Ah, my first lover, and my vanished youth!)

Bride:

Almost I dread this night. My senses fail me.
How shall I dare to clasp a thing so dear?
Many have feared your name, but I your beauty
Lord of my life, be gentle to my fear!

Younger Sisters:

In the softest silk is our sister dressed,
With silver and rubies upon her breast,
Where a dearer treasure to-night will rest.

Dancing Girls:

See! his hair is like silk, and his teeth are whiter
Than whitest of jasmin flowers. Pity they marry him thus.
I would change my jewels against his caresses.
Verily, sisters, this marriage is greatly a loss to us!

Bride:

Would that the music ceased and the night drew round us,
With solitude, shadow, and sound of closing doors,
So that our lips might meet and our beings mingle,
While mine drank deep of the essence, beloved, of yours.

Passing Mendicant:

Out of the joy of your marriage feast,
Oh, brothers, be good to me,
The way is long and the Shrine is far,
Where my weary feet would be.
And feasting is always somewhat sad
To those outside the door —
Still; Love is only a dream, and Life
Itself is hardly more!

Morsellin Khan

Husband: I take thee to my wedded wife, to have and to hold from this day forward, for better for worse, for richer for poorer, in sickness and in health, to love and to cherish, till death us do part, according to God's holy ordinance; and thereto I plight thee my troth.

Wife: I take thee to my wedded husband, to have and to hold from this day forward, for better for worse, for richer for poorer, in sickness and in health, to love, cherish, and to obey, till death us do part, according to God's holy ordinance; and thereto I give thee my troth.

Husband: With this ring I thee wed, with my body I thee worship, with all my worldly goods I thee endow:...

The Book of Common Prayer ~

54

THE INSTITUTION OF MARRIAGE is prescribed only for the human race. In this creation, there is no prescribed institution of marriage for either higher beings or lower generations...
Marriage is institutionalised for human beings because they stand at the crossroads of the creation. They can either evolve for higher level or sink into lower...Being at the crossroad of creation, the human race has a duty to improve rather than degenerate...

The question of marriage, according to the Vedic tradition, is settled on the principle that one accepts the other for life. Whatever the life has to offer, it must be shared in union and thus the matrimonial relation is unbreakable. There is no provision for divorce...

To keep looking round for objects of passion is a disgraceful act for the dignity of man; then why provide such opportunities for self-destruction?

Shantanand Saraswati

The love of self always brings dissatisfaction, for the self is not made to be loved; the self is made to love. The first condition of love is to forget oneself. One cannot love another and oneself at the same time, and if one says, 'If you give me something I will give you something in return', that is another kind of love, it is more like business.

Inayat Khan

Those who have love in their hearts and reason in their minds act in unison for they feed on bliss; but those whose heart says one thing and their mind says another, they feed on pleasure and pain. They have not realised love or unity.

Shantanand Saraswati

No one can involve me in what is de-
basing ~nor can I be wroth with my kins-
man and hate him. For we have come into
being for co-operation, as have the feet, the
hands, the eyelids, the rows of upper and
lower teeth. Therefore to thwart one another
is against Nature; and we do thwart one
another by showing resentment and aversion.

Marcus Aurelius

We may, if we choose, make the worst of
one another. Everyone has his weak points;
everyone has his faults. We may make the
worst of these; we may fix our attention constantly on these. But we may also make the
best of one another. By loving whatever is
loveable in those around us, love will flow back
from them to us, and life will become a pleasure instead of a pain; and earth will become
like heaven; and we shall become not unworthy
followers of Him whose name is Love.

Dean Stanley

THE RELATIONSHIP of man and woman is such that if a man knows that the woman is entirely for him in body, mind and heart then he will take full responsibility and do anything and everything possible and sacrifice all for her... It is curious that women today although naturally made to surrender to a man, yet want to retain some independence and this feeling of surrendering and yet retaining a little independence for themselves creates a mixture, an impurity and the proper surrender is not made possible and this creates disbelief between the parties. If one wants to surrender only half way and reserve the right of being independent then where do they meet? In fact the meeting does not take place. They never get related as man and woman. Relationship is not materialised. SURRENDER alone is the relation ...

If a woman wants to keep independence she will get loneliness, if she surrenders, she gets it all.

Shantanand Saraswati

THE OBJECT OF UNITY is the resolution to face all situations in unison, come what may. This is the liberating resolve which seeks no promise of a happy, comfortable and trouble-free harmonious life. Not all such marriages secure total happiness. Many have suffered unexpected difficulties. The achievement is... that they would never think of leaving the other to suffer alone. Those who plan union only for happiness and pleasure will sooner or later separate in vain search for another chance. The idea is that just as the shadow never leaves the individual, the partner in such union can never leave the partner. They are partners in truth, that is in all circumstances. They are not fair weather partners. Man is by nature standing at the crossroads of nature and must be ready to accept the breeze of pleasure and the storm of miseries, and do so together. This togetherness is the real gain, not the promise of a happy life.

Shantanand Saraswati

With regard to marriage, it is plain that
it is in accordance with reason, if the
desire of connection is engendered not
merely by external form, but by a love of
begetting children and wisely educating
them; and if, in addition, the love both of
the husband and wife has for its cause
not external form merely, but chiefly
liberty of mind.

Baruch Spinoza

MOTHERHOOD

He who has all forms, the
golden one, all knowing;
The final goal, the only light, heat
                                    giving,
The thousand-rayed, the hundredfold
                                    revolving,
Yon sun arises as the life of creatures.

Prasna Upanishad

From me the world is born, in me it
exists, in me it dissolves, as jars return
to clay, waves to water and bracelets
to gold.

Bhagavad Gita

I am the family face;
Flesh perishes, I live on
Through time to times anon
And leaping from place to place
Over oblivion.

Thomas Hardy

She thought:

How can he be united with me after producing me from himself? Well, let me hide myself. She became a cow, the other became a bull and was united with her; from that cows were born. The one became a mare, the other a stallion; the one became a she-ass, the other became a he-ass and was united with her, from that one-hoofed animals were born. The one became a she-goat, the other a he-goat, the one became a ewe, the other became a ram and was united with her, from that goats and sheep were born. Thus did he project everything that exists in pairs...

Brihadaranyaka Upanishad

In the dark womb where I began
My mothers life made me a man.
Through all the months of human birth
Her beauty fed my common earth.
I cannot see, nor breathe, nor stir,
But through the death of some of her.

John Masefield

A woman's life is quite different from a man's. God has ordered it so. A man is the same from the time of his circumcision to the time of his withering. He is the same before he has sought out a woman for the first time, and afterwards. But the day when a woman enjoys her first love cuts her in two. She becomes another woman on that day. The man is the same after his first love as he was before. The woman is from the day of her first love another. That continues so all through life. The man spends a night by a woman and goes away. His life and body are always the same. The woman conceives. As a mother she is another person than the woman without child. She carries the print of the night nine months long in her body. Something grows. Something grows into her life that never again departs from it. She is a mother. She is and remains a mother even though her child die, though all her children die. For at one time she carried the child under her heart. And it does not go out of her heart ever again. Not even when it is dead. And this the man does not know; he knows nothing. He does not know the difference before love and after love, before motherhood and after motherhood. Only a woman can know that and speak of that.

Frobenius

A little breeze blew over the sea,
  And it came from far away,
  Across the fields of millet and rice
All warm with sunshine and sweet with spice,
  It lifted his curls and kissed him thrice,
    As upon the deck he lay.

  It said, "Oh, idle upon the sea,
    Awake and with sleep have done,
    Haul up the widest sail of the prow,
    And come with me to the rice fields
                          now,
  She longs, oh, how can I tell you how
To show you your first-born son!"

Sampan Song

65

And, at the last, there began, anone
A lady for to sing right womanly...

A clear voice made to comfort and incite,
Lovely and peaceful as a moonlit deep,
A voice to make the eyes of strong men weep
With sudden overflow of great delight;
A voice to dream of in the calm of night...

Chaucer

SWEET AND LOW

Sweet and low, sweet and low, Wind of the west-ern sea......,
Low, low, breathe and blow, Wind of the west-ern sea..., Over the roll - ing
wa-ters go, Come from the dy-ing moon and blow, Blow him a-gain to
me..... While my lit-tle one, while my pret-ty one sleeps...........

B. Marston

66

EVERYONE

suddenly burst out singing;
And I was filled with such delight
As prisoned birds must find in freedom
Winging wildly across the white
Orchards and dark green fields; on; on;
and out of sight.

Everyone's voice was suddenly lifted,
And beauty came like the setting sun.
My heart was shaken with tears, and horror
Drifted away.... O, but every one
Was a bird; and the song was wordless;
the singing will never be done.

Siegfried Sassoon

And a woman who held a babe against her bosom said,
Speak to us of Children.
And he said:

YOUR CHILDREN
are not your children. They are the
sons and daughters of Life's longing for
itself. They come through you but not from
you. And though they are with you yet
THEY BELONG NOT TO YOU
You may give them your love but not your
thoughts, For they have their own thoughts. You
may house their bodies but not their souls, For
their souls dwell in the house of tomorrow, which
you cannot visit, not even in your dreams.
You may strive to be like them, but seek not to make
them like you. For life goes not backward nor tarries
with yesterday. You are the bows from which your
children as living arrows are sent forth. The archer
sees the mark upon the path of the infinite, and He
bends you with His might that His arrows may
go swift and far. Let your bending in the Archer's
hand be for gladness; for even as He loves the
arrow that flies, so He loves also the
BOW THAT IS
STABLE.

Khalil Gibran

was a lovely morning with fleeting clouds and a clear blue sky. It had rained, and the air was clean. Every leaf was new and the dreary winter was over; each leaf knew, in the sparkling sunshine, that it had no relation to last years spring. The sun shone through the new leaves, shedding a soft green light on the wet path that led through the woods to the main road that went to the big city. There were children playing about, but they never looked at that lovely spring day. They had no need to look, for they were the spring. Their laughter and their play were part of the tree, the leaf and the flower. You felt this. You didn't imagine it. It was as though the leaves and the flowers were taking part in the laughter, in the shouting, and in the balloon that went by. Every blade of grass, and the yellow dandelion, and the tender leaf that was so vulnerable, were all part of the children, and the children were part of the whole earth. Krishnamurti

NOW AS I WAS YOUNG

and easy under the apple boughs
About the lilting house and happy as the
grass was green,
The night above the dingle starry.
Time let me hail and climb
Golden in the heydays of his eyes,
And honoured among wagons I was prince
of the apple towns
And once below a time I lordly had the
trees and leaves
Trail with daisies and barley
Down the rivers of the windfall light.

And as I was green and carefree, famous
among the barns
About the happy yard and singing as the
farm was home,
In the sun that is young once only,
Time let me play and be

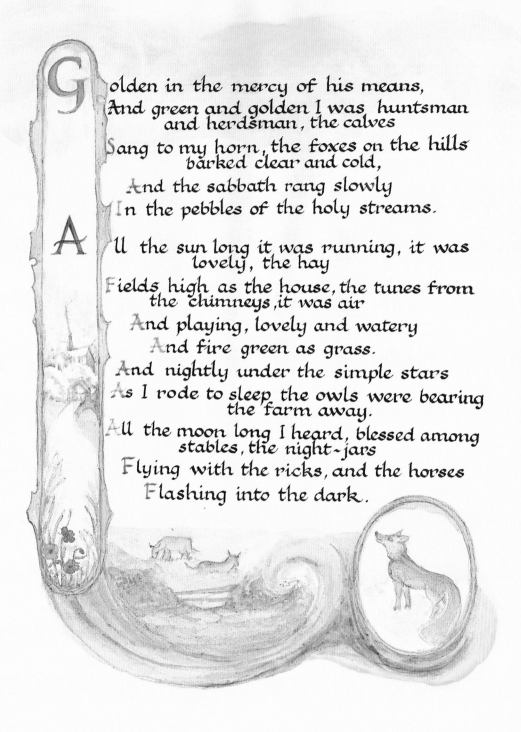

Golden in the mercy of his means,
And green and golden I was huntsman
    and herdsman, the calves
Sang to my horn, the foxes on the hills
    barked clear and cold,
    And the sabbath rang slowly
In the pebbles of the holy streams.

All the sun long it was running, it was
    lovely, the hay
Fields high as the house, the tunes from
    the chimneys, it was air
    And playing, lovely and watery
    And fire green as grass.
And nightly under the simple stars
As I rode to sleep the owls were bearing
    the farm away.
All the moon long I heard, blessed among
    stables, the night-jars
    Flying with the ricks, and the horses
    Flashing into the dark.

71

And then to awake, and the farm, like a
wanderer white
With the dew, come back, the cock on his
shoulder: it was all
SHINING
it was Adam and maiden,
The sky gathered again
And the sun grew round that very day.
o it must have been after the birth of the
SIMPLE LIGHT

In the first, spinning place, the spellbound
horses walking warm
Out of the whinnying green stable
On to the

FIELDS OF PRAISE

Dylan Thomas

72

ON
THE SEASHORE
OF ENDLESS WORLDS

children meet. The infinite sky is
motionless overhead and the restless
water is boisterous. On the seashore of endless worlds the children meet with shouts and
dances. They build their houses with sand and
they play with empty shells. With withered leaves
they weave their boats and smilingly float them
on the vast deep. Children have their play on the
seashore of worlds.

Rabindranath Tagore

 CHILD is very much like a green bamboo shoot which can be bent in any way if a little heat and oil is applied. Having bent it, one needs to maintain that for a few days and it would become permanent. If bamboo gets mature and turns yellow, then it would not be possible. It might break rather than bend. The child is tender and ready to receive any form, good or bad, whatever is provided. If one can provide a good emotional, spiritual or devotional knowledge, the child will pick them up and use them in his life.

RELATIONS between parents and their children are harmoniously regulated through love and discipline. Love gives them support for development and discipline keeps them within the established orders of the family and society. The nature of the child is very tender and it is likely to take any shape or form and it can be distorted very quickly as well. If too much love is provided the child may turn wilful and if too much discipline is enforced, then he

may close in or resent from inside. Thus, he
needs them both, just in right measure.

The child is pliable like the refined clay of a
potter who is about to throw a pot. The potter
uses both his hands, one inside and the other
outside. The hand inside is the hand of love,
which gives support for expansion, and the hand
outside is the hand of discipline, which keeps a
firm control on the expansion within the required form. It is prescriptive and regulative
in action. The parents have to act like a
potter.

They must have the concept of a good civil-
-ised and cultured being which they wish the
child to evolve into, and they must support
with love from within for the expansion of
the child and must regulate the child to
conform to the norms of universal nature
with restrictive, prescriptive or punitive
force. This will create a good character and
a pleasant being.

Shantanand Saraswati

I LEARNED FROM MY MOTHER

just what it meant to cope with a household so that everything worked like clockwork. She showed me how to iron a man's shirt and to press embroidery without damaging it. Large flat-irons were heated over the fire and I was let in on the secret of how to give a special finish to linen by putting just enough candle wax to cover a sixpenny piece on the iron. The whole house was not just cleaned daily and weekly: a great annual spring clean was intended to get to all those parts which other cleaning could not reach. Carpets were taken up and beaten. The mahogany furniture was washed down with warm water and vinegar before being repolished. Since this was also the time of the annual stocktaking in the shop, there was hardly time to draw breath...

My mother was a great rock of family stability. Like many people who live for others, she made possible all that her husband and daughters did. Her life was not an easy one. Although in later years I would speak more readily of my father's political influence on me, it was from her that I inherited the ability to organise and combine so many different duties of an active life.

Margaret Thatcher

AT NINE THEY STOPPED WORK

and sang, as usual, before they went to bed. No one but Beth could get much music out of the old piano; but she had a way of softly touching the keys, and making a pleasant accompaniment to the simple songs they sang. Meg had a voice like a flute, and she and her mother led the little choir. Amy chirped like a cricket, and Jo wandered through the airs at her own sweet will, always coming out at the wrong place with a crook or a quaver that spoilt the pensive tune. They had always done this, and it had become a household custom, for the mother was a born singer. The first sound in the morning was her voice, as she went about the house singing like a lark, and the last sound at night was the same cheery sound, for the girls never grew too old for that familiar lullaby *Louisa M. Alcott*

It is written in the Book of Wisdom that 'as is the rising sun to the world, so is a good woman to her household'. The rising sun...frees the world from horror of darkness, brings in the pleasant and joyous light of the day...and imparts comfort, sustenance, light, life and warmth to every creature on this earth. Even so should your kindness and goodness and virtue introduce into your household the brightness and charm which the morning rays of the sun bestow upon the world... *Robert Grosseteste*

77

SOFTLY, in the dusk, a woman is singing to me;
Taking me back down the vista of years, till I see
A child sitting under the piano, in the boom of
        the tingling strings
And pressing the small, poised feet of a mother
        who smiles as she sings.

In spite of myself, the insidious mastery of song
Betrays me back, till the heart of me weeps to
        belong
To the old Sunday evenings at home, with winter
        outside
And hymns in the cosy parlour, the tinkling piano
        our guide.

So now it is vain for the singer to burst into clamour
With the great black piano appassionato. The glamour
Of childish days is upon me, my manhood is cast
Down in the flood of remembrance, I weep like a
        child for the past. D. H. Lawrence

He who binds to himself a Joy
Does the winged life destroy;
He who kisses the Joy as it flies,
Lives in Eternity's sunrise.
William Blake –

ALTHOUGH we have been made to believe
that if we let go we will end up with nothing,
life itself reveals again and again the opposite:
that letting go is the path to real freedom.
Just as when the waves lash at the shore, the
rocks suffer no damage but are sculpted and
eroded into beautiful shapes, so our characters
can be molded and our rough edges worn smooth
by changes. Through weathering changes we
can learn how to develop a gentle but unshake-
able composure. Our confidence in ourselves
grows, and becomes so much greater that goodness and compassion begin naturally to radiate
out from us and bring joy to others. That goodness
is what survives death, a fundamental goodness
that is in everyone of us.

Sogyal Rinpoche

Who can find a virtuous woman? for her price is far above rubies. ✦ The heart of her husband doth safely trust in her, so that he shall have no need of spoil. ✦ She will do him good and not evil all the days of her life. ✦ She seeketh wool, and flax, and worketh willingly with her hands. ✦ She is like the merchants' ships; she bringeth her food from afar. ✦ She riseth also while it is yet night, and giveth meat to her household, and a portion to her maidens. ✦ She considereth a field, and buyeth it; with the fruit of her hands she planteth a vineyard. ✦ She girdeth her loins with strength, and strengtheneth her arms. ✦ She perceiveth that her merchandise is good: her candle goeth not out by night ✦ She layeth her hands to the spindle, and her hands hold the distaff. ✦ She stretcheth out her hand to the poor; yea, she reacheth forth her hands to the needy. ✦ She is not afraid of the snow for her household; for all her household are clothed with scarlet. ✦ She maketh herself coverings of tapestry: her clothing is silk and purple. ✦ Her husband is known in the gates, when he sitteth among the elders of the land. ✦ She maketh fine linen, and selleth it; and delivereth girdles unto the merchant. ✦ Strength and honour are her clothing; and she shall rejoice in time to come. ✦ She openeth her mouth with wisdom; and in her tongue is the law of kindness. ✦ She looketh well to the ways of her household, and eateth not the bread of idleness. ✦ Her children arise up, and call her blessed; her husband also, and he praiseth her ✦ Many daughters have done virtuously, but thou excellest them all. ✦ Favour is deceitful, and beauty is vain: but a woman that feareth the LORD, she shall be praised. ✦ Give her of the fruit of her hands; and let her own works praise her in the gates. ✦   Ecclesiastes

HOME

**EEPLY** embedded in humankind is the desire to found a home, a shelter where one can feel safe and secure. Whether we dream of a country cottage, a mansion or a simple room, sooner or later we shall choose four walls and begin to gather possessions about us.

It is in the gift of woman to endow her surroundings with beauty and peace by remembering that every task is an act of service to those surrounding her.

Today, the daily round may also encompass work in city and office; nonetheless, the opportunity to connect with the subtle and spiritual worlds is ever present, and can lead, as in the account of the life of Mother Maria, to great acts of love and compassion.

Mine be a cot beside a hill;
A beehive's hum shall soothe my ear;
A willowy brook that turns a mill
With many a fall, shall linger near.

The swallow, oft, beneath my thatch
Shall twitter, from her clay-built nest;
Oft shall the pilgrim lift the latch
And share my meal, a welcome guest.

Around my ivied porch shall spring,
Each fragrant flower that drinks the dew;
And Lucy, at her wheel, shall sing
In russet gown and apron blue.

The village-church among the trees,
Where first our marriage vows were given,
With merry peals shall swell the breeze
And point with taper spire to Heaven.

Samuel Rogers ~

Portrait of a House

THE HOUSE THAT WE LIVE IN was built in a place
That was once a mere cube of unoccupied space;
And the birds who flew through it and passed on their way
Would collide with a wall or a window today.

The rooms in the house are of medium size,
The sort that an ant would regard with surprise;
While a whale could express no opinion at all,
For his bulk would prevent him from passing the hall.

The stairs are arranged with such exquisite skill
That a person can climb or descend them at will,
And the absence of rain from the attics is proof
That the architect thought of supplying a roof.

Of the doors and the windows our only complaint
Is the fact that you cant see the wood for the paint;
A trouble with which we've decided to deal
By allowing the paint to continue to peel.

The chairs and the tables are perfectly tame,
And to speak of them harshly is rather a shame;

But nevertheless I am bound to remark
On their savage resistance when bumped in the dark.

In the kitchen, in spite of its tropical clime,
Two cats and a cook spend the whole of their time.
The cats have been known to meander about,
But the cook is a fixture and never goes out.

It is said that mysterious sounds may be heard
In the house when it's empty, but this is absurd.
If you've gone there to listen, it's clear to a dunce
That the house will have ceased to be empty at once.

We've a spare room prepared for the casual guest,
But it really is not what the name would suggest;
For although its a room, it is never to spare,
As someone or other is constantly there.

I have made it quite clear that our chosen abode
Is different from all of the rest of the road ~
What a beautiful house for play, dinner and slumber!
And yet to the postman it's only a number.

E. V. Rieu

WHAT IS A HOME?

After all, married or not, a lady is expected to establish a home. This is difficult for some unmarried ladies; they imagine home must include a man and possibly children; and some will go on living out of suitcases for years, fearing to gather anything with a settled look around them. This is bad thinking, of course. One lives in the present; and the present for any lady involves looking after some small part of her village or town or city, some small part of the creation - making it as fitting and elegant as possible, in relation to herself at the centre of it...
Home has nothing to do with possessions. Home can be a palace or a hut; and visitors may feel more at home under a tree than in some homes.

So what is home?

Perhaps we need not define home. It is one of those sounds which resonate deeply within all human experience. We just remember that there are homes at all levels, in all worlds.

Sheila Rosenberg

Lord of all pots and pans and tins, since I've no
time to be
A saint by doing lovely things, or watching late
with Thee,
Or dreaming in the twilight, or storming heaven's
gates,
Make me a saint by getting meals and washing up
the plates

Although I must have Martha's hands, I have a Mary
mind;
And when I black the boots and shoes, Thy sandals,
Lord, I find;
I think of how they trod the earth, each time I
scrub the floor.
Accept this meditation, Lord, I haven't time for more.

Warm all the kitchen with Thy love and light it
with Thy peace;
Forgive me all my worryings and make all
grumbling cease;
Thou who didst love to give men food ~ in room or
by the sea ~
Accept this service that I do, I do it unto Thee.

Anon

86

God ~ let me be aware.
Let me not stumble blindly down the ways,
Just getting somehow safely through the days,
Not even groping for another hand,
Not even wondering why it all was planned,
Eyes to the ground unseeking for the light,
Soul never aching for a wild-winged flight,
Please, keep me eager just to do my share.
God ~ let me be aware.

God ~ let me be aware.
Stab my soul fiercely with others' pain,
Let me walk seeing horror and stain,
Let my hands, groping, find other hands,
Give me the heart that divines, understands.
Give me the courage, wounded, to fight,
Flood me with knowledge, drench me in light.
Please, keep me eager just to do my share.
God ~ let me be aware.

Miriam Teichner

It all started when the tumble-dryer broke down. I had to do that quaint old thing with the line and the clothes pins. As I was taking down all the crisp laundry, smelling of April sunshine, it suddenly occurred to me that there is a whole generation of working women who are missing out on the sensory pleasures of domesticity. They run from home to office, coping with unreliable domestic help, meting out quality time to querulous toddlers, phoning home between meetings to ask after a sick child – and never have time to smell the laundry along the way.

Janet Daley

Stocking and shirt
Can trip and prance
Though nobody's in them
To make them dance.

See how they waltz
Or minuet,
Watch the petticoat
Pirouette.

This is the dance
Of stocking and shirt,
When the wind puts on
The white lace skirt.

Old clothes and young clothes
Dance together
Twirling and whirling
In the mad March weather.

88

'Come!' cried the wind
To stocking and shirt
'Away!' cries the wind
To blouse and skirt.

Then clothes and wind
All pull together,
Tugging like mad
In the mad March weather.

Across the garden
They suddenly fly
And over the far hedge
High, high, high.

'Stop!' cries the housewife,
But all too late
Her clothes have passed
The furthest gate.

They are gone for ever
In the bright blue sky,
And only the handkerchiefs
Wave goodbye.

                    James Reeves

Mom was not much for cooking but on occasion she would surprise us. Her favourite dishes were rice pudding with raisins, veal steak and gravy, popcorn with lots of butter, fruit salad made with jello and canned fruit, and chocolate fudge she made to perfection. One day while living on Smith Street, Mom decided to bake bread. Such excitement it caused! She had made bread before but for some reason this particular day stands out above all others. In fact I can even remember the huge yellow earthenware bowl she used to mix the dough in.It was big enough to nestle the round lump of bouncy dough in its protecting depths, yet left room for rising. We watched it gradually heave under the damp teatowel. Mother punched it down and it rose again. Finally she set it on the back attic stairs where the heat was just right for a good rise. My but that bread took a long time to make.

We didn't have an oven but by prearrangement the coal-and-wood stove downstairs in Alma's kitchen was hot and ready to receive those loaves. It was agony to wait the hour required for baking but finally out came those huge golden loaves, ready to have their crisp crusts kissed with butter to make them soft and tender. I suppose there were some cautioning words about how new bread can give you a tummy ache but after much pleading we finally got to gobble up those thick slices still warm with the butter melting almost as soon as it was applied. Mom was, without a doubt, the world's best bread-maker.

Belle Curd

90

Hands making bread
immersed in sticky dough
patiently pummelling
kneading and stretching
until it is smooth and clean
then waiting as the yeast
in warmth and silence
inflates the grain ~
and kneading again.

or an underground bakery
with blazing lights
and blaring radio
at two in the morning ~
my Breton neighbours.

I imagine an uncluttered kitchen
with scrubbed pine table
and windows open to a country garden
where the smell of fresh loaves
lingers all week long

Hands breaking bread
the mother at a seder
the priest at an altar
the volunteer at a refugee camp
children on a picnic
an old man eating alone
with solemn dignity
asking a blessing
toddlers feeding the ducks
are all one bread, one body
and the yeast
rising within us
lets the spirit through.
Barbara Moss

IT WAS A CLEAR SUNNY DAY.
The midafternoon sun shone directly on some
of the flowerpots that hung from the
eaves of the roof around the corridor
and projected their shadows on the
north and east walls of the patio.
The combination of intense yellow
sunlight, the massive black shadows
create of the pots, and the lovely, delicate,
such an bare shadows of the frail flower-
exquisite ing plants that grew in them
effect. was stunning. Someone with
"The nagual a keen eye for balance
woman has and order had pruned
done that," those plants to
don Juan said as
if reading my thoughts.
"She gazes at these
shadows in the afternoons.
The thought of her gazing
at shadows in the after-
noons had a swift and devast-
ating effect on me. The intense
yellow light of that hour, the quietness
of that town, and the affection that I felt
for the nagual woman conjured up for me in one
instant all the solitude of the warriors' endless
path. Carlos Castaneda

OF ALL THE VIRTUES PROPER TO A WOMAN

the most vital to the fulfilment of her function is generosity. This is necessary all the time. She may be giving physical things: in times of economic distress, for example, to ensure that husband and children do not go without. She may be giving time: and must not seek some theoretical indulgence like "time for myself." She may be called upon to give a welcome: this most days, to husband or child returning from the office or school, quite apart from the welcome for trades-men, neighbours, and other visitors. Most of all, she will be giving of her own substance, more often than she realises. All this giving is part of her function. How differently is the function per-formed when the giving is large and generous.

Sheila Rosenberg

I have passed all my days in London, until I have formed as many and intense local attachments as any of you mountaineers can have done with nature. The lighted shops of the Strand and Fleet Street, the innumerable trades, tradesmen and customers, coaches, wagons, playhouses, all the bustle and wickedness round about Covent Garden, the very women of the Town, the watchmen, drunken scenes, rattles~life awake, if you awake, at all hours of the night, the impossibility of being dull in Fleet Street, the crowds, the very dirt and mud, the sun shining upon houses and pavements, the print shops, the old book~stalls, parsons cheap'ning books, coffee houses, steams of soups from kitchens, the pantomimes, London itself a pantomime and masquerade, ~ all these things work themselves into my mind and feed me, without a power of satiating me. The wonder of these sights impells me into night-walks about her crowded streets, and I often shed tears in the Motley Strand from the fulness of joy at so much life.

Charles Lamb

O World invisible, we view thee,
 O World intangible, we touch thee,
O World unknowable, we know thee,
 Inapprehensible, we clutch thee!

Does the fish soar to find the ocean,
 The eagle plunge to find the air ~
 That we ask of the stars in motion
 If they have rumour of thee there?

Not where the wheeling systems darken,
And our benumbed conceiving soars! ~
The drift of pinions, would we hearken,
Beats on our own clay-shuttered doors.

The angels keep their ancient places; ~
 Turn but a stone, and start a wing!
 'Tis ye, 'tis your estrangèd faces
 That miss the many-splendoured thing.

But (when so sad thou canst not sadder)
 Cry; ~ and upon thy so sore loss
 Shall shine the traffic of Jacob's ladder
Pitched betwixt Heaven and Charing Cross.

Yea, in the night, my Soul, my daughter,
 Cry; ~ clinging Heaven by the hems;
 And lo, Christ walking on the water,
 Not of Gennesareth, but Thames!

                    Francis Thompson ~

95

The many Russian refugees in France in those days were stateless persons, many of them poverty-stricken, without privilege, without claim on any of the services which the country provided for the poor. Mother Maria worked among the poorest. She discovered that Russians who contracted tubercolosis were lying in a filthy hovel on the banks of the Seine into which the Paris police used to throw those syphilitic wrecks which they picked up along the riverside. With ten francs in her pocket she bought a chateau and opened a sanatorium.

Then she found that there were hundreds of Russians in lunatic asylums all over Europe. They had just "disappeared" in these institutions, where no questions were asked about them. She raised a public outcry and got many of them released. In those days the Russian congregations in and around Paris were living examples of what the early apostolic communities must have been. They were real homes for the poor and the unwanted. Russians living in tenements could find there comfort and friendship. The Churches had their own labour exchanges, clinics and many other services, and the convent, over which Mother Maria presided, was central to their life.

When the German occupation took place Mother Maria summoned her chaplain and told him that she felt that her particular duty was to render all possible assistance to persecuted Jews. She knew that this would mean imprisonment and probably death, and she gave him the option of leaving. He refused. For a month the convent was a haven for Jews. Women and children were hidden within its walls.

Money poured in to enable them to escape from France and hundreds were got away. At the end of a month the Gestapo came. Mother Maria was arrested and sent to the concentration camp at Ravensbruck. Her chaplain was sent to Buchenwald, where he died of starvation and overwork.

The story of her life in the camp is only now being pieced together. She was known even to the guards as "that wonderful Russian nun," and it is doubtful whether they had any intention of killing her. She had been there two and a half years when a new block of buildings was erected in the camp, and the prisoners were told that these were to be hot baths. A day came when a few dozen prisoners from the women's quarters were lined up outside the buildings. One girl became hysterical. Mother Maria, who had not been selected, came up to her. "Don't be frightened," she said. "Look, I shall take your turn," and in line with the rest, she passed through the doors. It was Good Friday, 1945.   Christian Newsletter

NATURE

IS ALWAYS AN UNFAILING FOUNTAIN OF INSPIRATION. TO CALM YOUR MIND, go for a walk at dawn in the park, or watch the dew on a rose in a garden. Lie on the ground and gaze up into the sky, and let your mind expand into its spaciousness. Let the sky outside awake a sky inside your mind. Stand by a stream and mingle your mind with its rushing; become one with its ceaseless sound. Sit by a waterfall and let its healing laughter purify your spirit. Walk on a beach and take the sea wind full and sweet against your face. Celebrate and use the beauty of moonlight to poise your mind. Sit by a lake or in a garden and, breathing quietly, let your mind fall silent as the moon comes up majestically and slowly in the cloudless night.

Everything can be used as an invitation to meditation. A smile, a face in the subway, the sight of a small flower growing in the crack of a cement pavement, a fall of rich cloth in a shop window, the way the sun lights up flower-pots on a window sill. Be alert for any sign of beauty or grace. Offer up every joy, be awake at all moments, to 'the news that is always arriving out of

SILENCE.

Sogyal Rinpoche

THESE
I HAVE LOVED

White plates and cups, clean - gleaming,
Ringed with blue lines ; and feathery, faery dust;
Wet roofs, beneath the lamp-light ; the strong crust
Of friendly bread ; and many-tasting food;
Rainbows; and the blue bitter smoke of wood;
And radiant raindrops couching in cool flowers;
And flowers themselves, that sway through sunny hours,
Dreaming of moths that drink them under the moon;
Then, the cool kindliness of sheets, that soon
Smooth away trouble; and the rough male kiss
Of blankets ; grainy wood; live hair that is
Shining and free; blue-massing clouds; the keen
Unpassioned beauty of a great machine;
The benison of hot water; furs to touch;
The good smell of old clothes; and other such~
The comfortable smell of friendly fingers,
Hair's fragrance, and the musty reek that lingers
About dead leaves and last year's ferns...

Rupert Brooke

99

When you were there, and you, and you,
Happiness crowned the night; I too,
Laughing and looking, one of all
I watched the quivering lamplight fall
On plate and flowers and pouring tea
And cup and cloth; and they and we
Flung all the dancing moments by
With jest and glitter. Lip and eye
Flashed on the glory, shone and cried,
Improvident, unmemoried;
And fitfully and like a flame
The light of laughter went and came
Proud in their careless transience moved
The changing faces that I loved.

Till suddenly, and otherwhence,
I looked upon your innocence;
For lifted clear and still and strange
From the dark woven flow of change
Under a vast and starless sky
I saw the immortal moment lie.
One instant I, and instant knew
As God knows all. And it and you
I, above Time, oh blind, could see
In witless immortality.
I saw the marble cup, the tea,
Hung on the air, an amber stream;
I saw the fire's unglittering gleam,

The painted flame, the frozen smoke
No more the flooding lamplight broke
On flying eyes and lips and hair;
But lay, but slept unbroken there,
On stiller flesh, and body breathless,
And lips and laughter stayed and deathless,
And words on which no silence grew,
Light was more alive than you.

For suddenly and otherwhence,
I looked on your magnificence.
I saw the stillness and the light,
And you august, immortal, white,
Holy and strange; and every glint
Posture and jest and thought and tint
Freed from the mask of transciency,
Triumphant in eternity,
Immote, immortal.   Rupert Brooke

N O W

stir the fire, and close the shutters fast.
Let fall the curtains, wheel the sofa round,
And, while the bubbling and loud-hissing urn
Throws up a steamy column, and the cups,
That cheer but not inebriate, wait on each,
So let us welcome peaceful evening in...
              William Cowper

At the top of the house the apples are laid in rows,
And the skylight lets the moonlight in, and those
Apples are deep-sea apples of green. There goes
A cloud on the moon in the autumn night.

A mouse in the wainscot scratches, and scratches,
            and then
There is no sound at the top of the house of men
Or mice; and the cloud is blown, and the moon again
Dapples the apples with deep-sea light.

They are lying in rows there, under the gloomy
            beams;
On the sagging floor; they gather the silver streams
Out of the moon, those moonlit apples of dreams,
And quiet is the steep stair under.

In the corridors under there is nothing but sleep,
And stiller than ever on orchard boughs they keep
Tryst with the moon, and deep is the silence, deep
On moon~washed apples of wonder.

John Drinkwater

And pluck till time and times are done
The silver apples of the moon,
The golden apples of the sun.

W.B. Yeats

THE ULTIMATE CAUSE OF THIS CREATION

IS LOVE, OUT OF WHICH THE INNER AND OUTER WORLD IS CREATED AND THE LOVE ITSELF TAKES ALL THESE DIFFERENT FORMS

AND ALL THE FORMS ARE RELATED TO AND THROUGH LOVE.

Shantanand Saraswati

MATURITY

WITH the passage of time one may come to a better understanding of the unfolding play.

Like a mountaineer approaching the summit, the traveller through life can view the extended vista with greater comprehension, glimpsing the essential unity and order that lie behind the apparent diversity.

With an awareness of the truth and beauty that rest at the root of all things, love and devotion are strengthened and mankind itself becomes the essential family.

From such a still and unified centre the elder lady will see and continue to meet the needs of those around her, will have the courage to face the difficulties presented to her, and will recognise the unchanging love which sustains all things.

THE OLD WOMAN

sat under the shade of the cottonwood tree by the creek and nodded her head, dozing a little. She was very old, so old that the wrinkles made little fine ridges all over her face and her eyes seemed hidden among the ridges like springs lost in a desert. But when a sand lizard ran among some rattleweed, brushing their stems and causing the pods to rattle in the windless air, she opened her eyes and they peered out from among the folds of skin, bright and glowing with life like two points of black desert opal sparkling in the sun. Eyes of the Fire she had been called long ago when she was seventeen and danced on the prairie while half a dozen fine young hunters pressed forward to woo her. But that was long, long ago...

North American Indian

YOUTH

is not entirely a time of life ~ it is a state of mind.

It is not wholly a matter of ripe cheeks, red lips or supple knees. It is a temper of the will, a quality of the imagination, a trigger of the emotions.

Nobody grows old merely by living a number of years. People grow old only by deserting their ideals. Each is as young as his faith, as old as his doubt, as young as his self-confidence, as old as his fears, as young as his hope, as old as his despair.

In the central place of every heart is a recording chamber. So long as it receives messages of hope, beauty, cheer, and courage, then so long are we young.

When you are no longer tuned to receive such messages your heart becomes covered with the snows of pessimism and the ice of cynicism then ~ and only then, are you grown old.

IN the plain of the world's dust like a great Sea,
The golden thunders of the Lion and the Honey~Bee
In the Spirit, held with the Sun a Colloquy

Where an old woman stood ~ thick Earthiness ~
Half Sun, half Clod,
A plant alive from the root, still blind with earth
And all the weight of Death and Birth.

She, in her primitive dress
Of clay, bent to her hives
And heard her sisters of the barren lives

Begin to stir… the Priestesses of the Gold Comb
Shaped by Darkness, and the Prophetesses
Who from a wingless pupa, spark of gold.

In the Dark, rose with gold bodies, bright as the Lion
And the trace of the Hand of God on ephemeral wings
To sing the great Hymn of Being to the lost:

"This Earth is the honey of all Beings, and all Beings
Are the honey of this Earth…O bright immortal Lover
That is incarnate in the body's earth ~
O bright immortal Lover Who is All!"

"This Water is the honey of all Beings, and all Beings
Are the honey of this Water… O the bright immortal
                              Lover
That is in water and that is the seed
Of Life…O bright immortal Lover Who is All!"

"This Fire is the honey of of all Beings, and all Beings
Are the honey of this Fire...O bright immortal Lover
That is in fire and shines in mortal speech ~
O bright immortal Lover Who is All!"

"This Air is the honey of all Beings, and all Beings
Are the honey of this Air,.. O bright immortal Lover
That is in air and in our Being's breath ~
O bright immortal Lover Who is All!"

"This Sun is the honey of all Beings, and all Beings
Are the honey of this Sun...O bright immortal Lover
That is the Sun and is our Being's sight ~
O bright immortal Lover Who is All!"

This Thunder is the honey of all Beings, and all Beings
Are the honey of this Thunder...O the bright
                                    immortal Lover
That is in thunder and all voices ~ the beasts' roar ~
Thunder of rising saps ~ the voice of Man!
O bright immortal Lover Who is All!"

This was the song that came from the small span
Of thin gold bodies shaped by the holy Dark...

And the old woman in her mortal dress of clay
(That plant alive from the root, still thick with earth)
Felt all the saps of Day...

                    Edith Sitwell

The sun upon the lake is low,
The wild birds hush their song,
The hills have evening's deepest glow,
Yet Leonard tarries long.
Now all whom varied toil and care
From home and love divide
In the calm sunset may repair
Each to the loved one's side.

The noble dame on turret high
 Who waits her gallant knight,
Looks to the western beam to spy
The flash of armour bright.
The village maid, with hand on brow
 The level ray to shade,
 Upon the footpath watches now
For Colin's darkening plaid.

Now to their mates the wild swans row,
By day they swam apart,
And to the thicket wanders slow
The hind beside the hart.
The woodlark at his partner's side
Twitters his closing song ~
All meet whom day and care divide,
But Leonard tarries long!

Sir Walter Scott

Let me grow lovely, growing old ~
So many fine things do;
Laces, and ivory, and gold,
And silks need not be new;
And there is healing in old trees,
Old streets a glamour hold
Why may not I, as well as these
Grow lovely, growing old.

Karle Wilson Baker

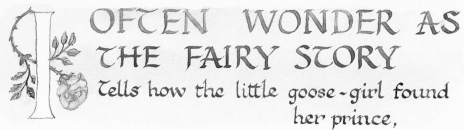

I OFTEN WONDER AS THE FAIRY STORY

Tells how the little goose-girl found
her prince,
Or of the widowed queen who stopped her carriage
And threw a rose down to the gangling dunce,
What is the meaning of this lucky marriage
Which lasts forever, it is often said,
Because I know too well such consummation
Is not a question of a double bed,
Or of the wedding bells and royal procession
With twenty major-domos at its head...

I mean the elder son and cherished sister
Know but the surface of each common day;
It takes the cunning eye of the rejected
To dip beneath the skin of shadow-play
And come into the meaning of a landscape.
I think that every bird and casual stone
Are syllables thrust down from some broad
language

That we must ravel out and make our own.
Yet who is ever turned towards that journey
Till deprivations riddle through the heart?
And so I praise the goose-girl and the scullion

Beside a midden and a refuse cart.

And yet all images for this completion
Somehow byepass its real ghostliness
Which can't be measured by a sweating finger
Or any salt and carnal nakedness.
Although two heads upon a single pillow
May be the metaphor that serves it best,
No lying down within a single moment
Will give the outward going any rest;
It's only when we reach beyond our pronouns
And come into ourselves that we are blest.
Is this the meaning of the lucky marriage
Which lasts forever, it is often said,
Between the goose-girl and the kitchen servant,
Who have no wedding ring or mutual bed?

                                    Thomas Blackburn

SHE laughed, and said:...I am only that bitter

sweet, a woman; and I want no more than what
every woman wants, the man she loves, and that
is thou. Aye! dost thou ask me, who and what I am?
Listen then, and I will tell thee. I am a bee, which
not like other bees, roams roving to flower after
flower, but confines itself exclusively to one. I am
a breeze, which not like other breezes blows fickle
and inconstant now hither and now thither, but is
fixed and ever steady, coming straight from Malaya
laden with the sandal of affection to lay it at thy
feet. I am only the echo of a voice which is thyself,
the shadow of a substance and the reflection of a
sun. I am like the other half of the god that carries
the moon upon his head, the twin, the duplicate and
counterpart of a deity who is thou. I am Rati, re-
joicing to find again the body of her husband, and
thou art Love himself returned to life whom I have
found. I am an essence of the ocean, but unlike it,
I hold within my heart not many pearls, but only
one, which is thyself. I am a wick, consuming in
thy flame, and like the music of a lute, I am a
thing wholly compounded of melodies and tones,
whose mood and being are dependant on the
player, who is thou. Art thou sad? then I am also:
art thou joyous? so am I: my soul is tossed

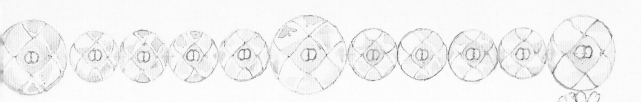

about, and hangs on thy smiling or thy sighing, as a criminal depends on the sentence of the judge. And like a crystal, I am colourless without thee, but ready on the instant to assume every tinge of the colour of thyself. Cast thy eyes upon me, and thou shalt see as in a glass thy every mood painted on the surface of my face...

W. H. Bain

IT is not for the sake of the husband that he is loved, but for one's own sake that he is loved. It is not for the sake of the wife that she is loved, but for one's own sake that she is loved. It is not for the sake of the sons that they are loved, but for one's own sake that they are loved...

It is not for the sake of all that all is loved, but for one's own sake that it is loved.

The Self, my dear, should be realised - should be heard of, reflected on and meditated upon. By the realisation of the Self, my dear, through hearing, reflection and meditation, all is known

Brihadaranyaka
Upanishad

reflection and meditation

LOOK AT MY WIFE AND SEE THE LONG JOURNEY that we have come.

Here we are together in the immensity of space, two people bound only by our love in the wastes of space and eternity. Love is the one thing we have against the implacable tyranny of time. Love is a strange force— like gravity that holds us together in the transcendant and will suffer no parting. It is a mystic power not of the world of material facts, a divine gift in compensation for our ephemeral life.   A. E. Falconar

When you make the two one and when you make the inner world as the outer, and the outer as the Inner and the above as the below, and when you make the male and the female into a single one, so that the male will not any more be a male and the female a female, when you put a single eye in the place of the many…and a single image in the place of all images, then you shall enter the

KINGDOM   Gospel of St. Thomas

116

THE SOLUTION TO THE MYSTERY OF BEING

is then to be found within or at the root of our own beings, within our own hearts. Every individual can find for himself the solution to the mystery, but he cannot convey that solution to others; he can only point the way that he himself has travelled, and affirm the reality of his knowledge. He factually knows the truth, for his own being is that truth.

The mind therefore, with its natural capacity for truth, partakes of this eternal unmoving. The will also by its nature longing for truth, can be granted its desire beyond movement and beyond time. Only a life dedicated by choice to the study and cultivation of truth is lived in the fullness of bliss beyond movement and beyond time.

Marsilio Ficino

I DO MY UTMOST

TO ATTAIN EMPTINESS;

I hold FIRMLY to stillness.

The myriad creatures all rise together
And I watch their return.

The teaming creatures
separate roots.

All return to their separate roots.

Returning to one's roots is known as
STILLNESS.

This is what is meant by returning to one's destiny.
Returning to one's destiny is known as the constant.
Knowledge of the constant is known as discernment.

Woe to him who wilfully innovates
While ignorant of the constant,
But should one act from knowledge of the constant
One's actions will lead to impartiality,

Impartiality to kingliness

Kingliness to heaven,

Heaven to the way,

The way to perpetuity,
And to the end of one's days one will
meet with no danger.

Tao Te Ching -

118

LET

your mind be quiet
realising the beauty of the
world, and the immense the boundless treasures
that it holds in store. All that you have within you, all that your heart desires, all that
your Nature so specially fits you for ~ that or
the counterpart of it waits embedded in the great
Whole,   for you. It will surely come to you.

Do not recklessly spill the
waters of your mind in this direction and in that, lest you
become like a spring lost and
dissipated in the desert.
But draw them together into a little
compass, and hold them still, so still;

And let them become clear, so clear, so
limpid, so mirror-like; At last the mountains
and the sky shall glass themselves in peaceful beauty, And the antelope shall descend to
drink, and to gaze at his reflected image,
and the lion to quench his thirst;

And Love himself shall come and bend over,
and catch his own likeness in you. Edward Carpenter

119

IF

there be RIGHTEOUSNESS in the heart,
there will be BEAUTY in the character.

If there be BEAUTY in the character
there will be HARMONY in the home.

If there be HARMONY in the home
there will be ORDER in the nation.

When there is ORDER in each nation
there will be PEACE in the world.

Chinese Proverb -

ACKNOWLEDGEMENTS

No creative work arises without the continuous and loyal support of the many. Family and friends alike sustain the conditions which allow the work to proceed, and one is aware of the unbroken chain reaching back through time to those others whose words are being used as a source of inspiration. Among these many helpers a few particular names stand out - David Boddy who gave and held direction, Eliane Wilson for her generous and unstinting encouragement, Nina Falwell for help with the initial research on language, my grandson, Sean Frisby for putting aside his own problems in order to proof-read and research facts, also Jonathan Self for his tireless background work. My daughter Carole, Christophe Chauveau and Dominique Bonnel deserve special mention for releasing me from more mundane daily tasks. Above all, I thank those special ladies who, by their behaviour and devotion are living examples of the finest qualities of womanhood, and without whom I would not have fully understood, in truth, the feminine nature.

For permission to include copyright material we gratefully acknowledge the following copyright holders:
Chief Rabbi Professor Jonathan Sacks for "Why Society Leads the Family" from The Times of 6th March 1995;
George Sassoon for 'Everyone Sang' by Siegfried Sassoon;
The estate of Carlos Castaneda for an extract from 'The Fire from Within' copyright 1984 by Carlos Castaneda;
The Times of 27th April 1995 for an article by Janet Daley 'It all started when the tumble drier broke down';

Wordsworth Editions for three extracts from 'The Prophet' by Kahlil Gibran.

Harper Collins USA for an extract from 'The Language of the Goddess' by Marija Gimbutas;

Harper Collins UK for an extract from 'The Downing Street Years' by Margaret Thatcher;

Princeton University Press for an extract from 'The Collected Works of C. G. Jung;

The Krishnamurti Foundation London for two extracts from 'The Only Revolution', copyright 1970 J. Krishnamurti.

Laurence Pollinger Ltd for 'Song of a Man who has come through' and 'Piano' from 'The Complete Poems of D. H. Lawrence;

The Society of Authors for the poem 'C.L.M." To His Mother" by John Masefield.;

John Johnson Ltd for 'Stocking and Shirt' from 'The Wandering Moon' by James Reeves, Heinemann 1950;

Honeyglen Publishing for an extract from 'Woman and Power in History' by Amaury de Riencourt;

Authors' Licensing and Collecting Society for 'Portrait of a House' by E. V. Rieu;

David Higham Associates for 'The Bee Keeper' by Edith Sitwell from 'Collected Poems' Sinclair Stevenson; and for 'Fern Hill' by Dylan Thomas from "Collected Poems' J. M. Dent;

Random House UK for extracts from 'The Tibetan Book of the Dead' by Sogyal Rimpoche;

Visva~Bharati for 'Light of my light' from 'Poems of Gitanjali' by Rabindranath Tagore;

Simon & Schuster for an extract from "The Healing of America' by Marianne Williamson.

E. J. Brill for an extract from 'The Gospel According to
Thomas';
Shepheard~Walwyn for an extract from 'The Letters of
Marsilio Ficino'.

The publisher has made every effort to trace copyright
owners. Where we have failed, we offer our apologies and
undertake to make proper acknowledgement in reprints.

INDEX OF AUTHORS

With Dates of Birth and Death, Countries of Birth and First Words ~

HAST THOU NEVER WATCHED THE BUBBLES ON THE SURFACE OF THE STREAM?

Dost thou not know how every bubble is like a little heaven, and glows for a moment with every colour of the sky, and bursts, but the sky remains? So it is with my picture. For like a bubble, it will burst as soon as painted, being only words: but the heaven which it shows thee in its mirror shall be thine, as long as life endures.